An Instant Guide to
MUSHROOMS &
OTHER FUNGI

The most familiar species of
North American mushrooms and fungi
described and illustrated in full color

ELEANOR LAWRENCE AND SUE HARNIESS

GRAMERCY BOOKS
NEW YORK

Warning Symbol

 Throughout the book this sign has been used to indicate that a mushroom is toxic, indigestible or has a highly disagreeable taste, and should never be eaten. Some mushrooms are deadly and therefore the reader is advised to take great care in identification of all types.

If in any doubt DO NOT EAT!

Always consult an expert!

This 2003 edition is published by Gramercy Books, an imprint of Random House Value Publishing, a division of Random House, Inc., New York.

Gramercy is a registered trademark and the colophon is a trademark of Random House, Inc.

Random House
New York • Toronto • London • Sydney • Auckland
www.randomhouse.com

Printed and bound in Singapore

A catalog record for this title is available from the Library of Congress.

ISBN 0-517-69115-9

10 9 8 7 6 5 4 3 2 1

Contents

Introduction

Fungi are amongst the most fascinating members of the vegetable kingdom. Traditionally regarded as plants, they are now placed by biologists in a kingdom of their own. Unlike green plants they contain no chlorophyll and cannot make their own food using the sun's energy. Instead they extract nourishment from the soil or from the wood or other material on which they live, causing it slowly to rot away. They are a most important part of the great cycle of life, releasing elements locked in dead animal and plant matter to be returned to the soil and used again.

There are many thousands of species of fungi, some so small they are only visible under the microscope. In this book we present a selection of the larger fungi, including many that are gathered for food and those deadly poisonous species that must be avoided at all costs.

Identifying fungi for the table requires great care. If you are a complete novice do not rely entirely on books but also get your finds identified by someone knowledgeable. A good way to start is to go on an organized mushroom hunt with a local mycological society or mushroom club.

Always check very carefully that a mushroom you think is edible corresponds in *all* respects to its description in the book. A difference in spore color, for example, could mean that you have gathered a poisonous species. **If you are at all unsure, do not eat it!** Before you go out collecting, look through the whole book and familiarize yourself with the better-known edible and poisonous species and note the ones that can be confused. Always gather the complete mushroom, including the very base of the stalk, so that you have all the parts needed to make an identification. Where possible also gather several of the same species at different stages in development. Collect mushrooms in a wide, flat-bottomed basket, not in plastic bags in which they become easily damaged and identifying features lost. Finally, when trying a new species for the first time, only eat a very little of it, as even edible mushrooms can cause illness and allergies in some susceptible people. Always keep one of the mushrooms in case it has to be identified by experts later.

All the mushrooms noted as edible in this book are common species that have been eaten for many years. Those not designated as either edible or poisonous should be regarded as inedible.

Very few mushrooms have familiar common names, and common names also vary widely from place to place and from book to book. Since it is so important to be sure exactly which mushroom one is dealing with the Latin name has also been included in each case. Although these may seem offputting at first it is well worth getting to know them as it is then much easier to check your finds with an expert or with other books.

How to use this book

The book has been divided into five main sections indicating the type of habitat in which certain mushrooms are most likely to be found. Each habitat is indicated by a different color band at the top of the page (see Contents page 7.) Some mushrooms grow in a close relationship with the roots of certain trees and are only found in association with them. Others, although they prefer a certain type of habitat, may also be found elsewhere. The five sections are:

Broadleaved Woodland
Most commonly found growing on the ground in broadleaved woodland or in association with broadleaved trees such as beech, birch and oak.

Coniferous Woodland
Most commonly found growing on the ground in coniferous woods or forests or in association with conifers such as pine and spruce.

Mixed Woodland
May be found growing on the ground in mixed woodland or in association with either coniferous or broadleaved trees.

Grasslands and Parks
Most typically found in grass or open situations, as in lawns, pasture, parks, gardens, roadsides, woodland glades, waste places, heaths, moors.

Growing on Wood
Growing directly on wood, as on living trees, stumps, cut timber, rotting wood, twigs and branches on the ground.

Within each main section fungi have been placed into subsections possessing certain identification features in common. These groups have been chosen to identify the species illustrated in this book only and do not necessarily reflect biological relationships. Within each color band these subsections are identified by symbols.

Identification features
Mushrooms are the fruiting bodies of certain sorts of fungi. The fungus lives for most of the year as a mass of thin threads known as a *mycelium*, which is sometimes visible as a cottony mass at the very base of the stalk. At the appropriate time of year, in late summer and fall for most mushrooms, this mycelium produces fruiting bodies containing spores by which the fungus propagates itself.

In some mushrooms the spores are borne on thin leaf-like *gills* on the underside of the cap (Fig. 1) in others (boletes, polypores and relatives) they are formed in close-packed tubes that take the place of the gills.

Important features to look for are the shape of the cap (Fig. 2,) whether the mushroom has a *ring* or *volva* on the stalk (see Fig. 1,) and how the gills are attached to the stalk (Fig. 3.) Not all mushrooms have all the features shown. Many mushrooms do not, for example, have a ring or a volva. In some mushrooms, such as cortinarias (corts,) the young gills are covered by a cobwebby veil, the *cortina*, which sometimes leaves traces on stalk and edge of cap. Always handle mushrooms carefully when gathering them to preserve the surface texture of the cap and stalk which are also useful in identification.

Fig. 1 *Left* Section through a gilled mushroom showing parts useful for identification. *Right* Immature mushroom showing how ring and volva are formed.

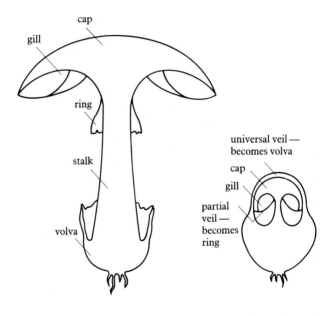

Fig. 2 Types of cap shape

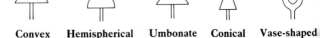

Convex   Hemispherical   Umbonate   Conical   Vase-shaped

Fig. 3 Types of gill attachment

Free   Adnexed   Adnate   Decurrent   Sinuate

Taking a spore print

The color of the spores is also an important identifying feature, helping to divide mushrooms into several large groups, and to distinguish between rather similar mushrooms belonging to different groups. To take a spore print the mushroom is cut off just below the cap and placed on a sheet of white paper (or black paper if you suspect you will get a white spore print.) A glass or a plastic bag is placed over it. After a period ranging from a few hours to a day, spores will drop from the gills or pores to make a print on the paper.

Identification symbols

Within each color band fungi with certain features in common have been grouped together, and each group is identified by the following symbol at the top of the page.

Fungi with teeth or ridges on undersurface, not gills or pores

    e.g. Black Trumpets, Chanterelle, Bear's Head Tooth.

Fungi with pores on underside of a cap or a bracket

    Central stem and rounded cap, growing on ground. These are the boletes.

    Fungi with very short or no stalk, or shelf-like, growing on wood, e.g. polypores, Turkey-tail.

Fungi with gills on underside of a cap or bracket

    No or very short stalk, or shelf-like, growing on wood, e.g. Oyster Mushroom.

11

Typical mushroom-like fungi with gills on the underside of a cap and a central stalk

 Small fragile mushrooms, generally no more than 6 cm:2½ in high with a delicate cap. Cap generally convex, hemispherical, or conical, e.g. mycenas, psilocybes.

 More robust mushrooms with gills that reach the stem (i.e. attached gills,) and no ring or volva, e.g. russulas, trichs, milk-caps, and many others.

 More robust mushrooms with attached gills, no volva, possessing a cobwebby veil (the cortina) over gills in young specimens, sometimes leaving a ring-like mark, or series of marks, on stalk, e.g. corts.

 More robust mushrooms with ring on stalk, no volva, and attached gills, e.g. agrocybes, Honey Mushroom, Gypsy.

 More robust mushrooms with no ring or volva on stem, gills do not reach stalk (free gills), e.g. Fawn Mushroom.

 Larger mushrooms with no ring on stem but which have a volva and free gills, e.g. volvariellas.

 Larger mushrooms with free gills, a ring on stalk, but no volva or with volva reduced to scales at base of stalk, e.g. agarics, some amanitas, lepiotas.

 Larger mushrooms with free gills and both ring and volva, e.g. some amanitas.

Fungi without teeth, gills or pores, fruitbodies not in

 typical mushroom shape, e.g. stinkhorn, morels, puffballs, earthstars, earth-balls, coral-fungi

After having determined, with the help of the color bands and the symbols, the section in which your mushroom is likely to be, look at the illustrated pages giving detailed descriptions of each species. The size is indicated on the colored band by measurements for cap diameter and length of stalk.

Four boxes provide information for identification. The first gives features which together with the illustration should enable you to distinguish that species from others illustrated in this book and

12

wherever possible from others which you might come across, especially poisonous species. The second box gives supplementary information to help identification, and notes on edibility or otherwise.

Distribution and habitat of the illustrated mushrooms are given in the third box, and the fourth box gives species with which they might be confused. Those in **bold type** are illustrated elsewhere in this book, those in roman type are not. The period during which the mushroom is most likely to appear is given under the boxes.

There are more than a thousand species of larger fungi in North America, and so you will inevitably find fungi not illustrated in this book. Nevertheless, you will be able to identify some of them to their family group or *genus*, such as *Agaricus*, *Russula* or *Lactarius*, by noting the spore color, type of attachment of the gills etc., and looking for similar species in these pages. However, **do not eat anything you have not identified precisely,** as a single genus can contain both edible and poisonous species.

Specimen page

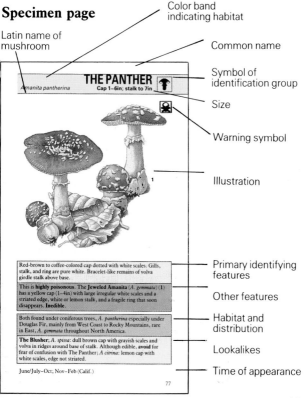

Color band indicating habitat

Latin name of mushroom

Common name

Symbol of identification group

Size

Warning symbol

Illustration

Primary identifying features

Other features

Habitat and distribution

Lookalikes

Time of appearance

Within illustration box:

THE PANTHER
Amanita pantherina   Cap 1–6in; stalk to 7in

Red-brown to coffee-colored cap dotted with white scales. Gills, stalk, and ring are pure white. Bracelet-like remains of volva girdle stalk above base.

This is **highly poisonous.** The **Jeweled Amanita** (*A. gemmata*) (1) has a yellow cap (1–6in) with large irregular white scales and a striated edge, white or lemon stalk, and a fragile ring that soon disappears. **Inedible.**

Both found under coniferous trees, *A. pantherina* especially under Douglas Fir, mainly from West Coast to Rocky Mountains, rare in East, *A. gemmata* throughout North America.

The Blusher; *A. spissa*: dull brown cap with grayish scales and volva in ridges around base of stalk. Although edible, **avoid** for fear of confusion with The Panther; *A. citrina*: lemon cap with white scales, edge not striated.

June/July–Oct; Nov–Feb (Calif.)

77

13

BLACK TRUMPET

Cap ¾–3¼in; ht 1½–5½in   *Craterellus fallax*

Blackish or dark gray-brown, narrow funnel-shaped cap with a flared wavy lip. Outer surface of cap is smooth or faintly ridged, the inner surface slightly scaly or velvety.

A small to medium-sized vase-shaped fungus with a short hollow stem and thin grayish flesh. Spore print yellowish-buff to pale orange. Fruity smell. Good to eat and can be dried and stored.

Under deciduous trees, especially beech and oak, often in troops. Throughout North America.

The similar *C. cornucopioides* has white spores, edible. The Blue Chanterelle (*Polyozellus multiplex*) is a cluster of blue to purple fan-shaped cups, under conifers, edible, most common on West Coast to Rocky Mountains, rarer in East.

July–November.

14

1

Convex matt rose-red cap eventually flattens out. Pores tiny, yellow, as is the smooth thick stalk. All parts slowly turn blue when bruised. Spore print olive-brown.

Very good to eat, with thick yellow flesh. The cap has a yellow rim and the yellow stalk is flushed rosy red except at the top. **Satan's Bolete** (*B. satanas*) (**1**) has a swollen stalk with a bright red network, pale gray cap and red pores. **Toxic**.

Under oak and aspen (also reported under pine.) Common in eastern North America from Nova Scotia to Georgia and Michigan. *B. satanas* generally occurs further south.

Other boletes, e.g. **Red-cracked Bolete, Bay Bolete, Bitter Bolete**. Do not eat any bolete with red or orange pores as **several are poisonous**.

June–October.

Rough stalk covered with hard small brown or black scales. Cap grayish-brown to dark brown, pores off-white to buff. Flesh unchanging when cut, or bruising slightly brownish.

A tall-stalked bolete with a cap dry, greasy, or sticky to the touch, sometimes becoming flat with a depression in center. Pores change from pale buff to grayish with age. Edible and good.

Very common, under broadleaved trees, especially birch. Widely distributed in North America.

Red-capped Scaber Stalk; *L. insigne*: tawny brown cap, under aspen or birch. Edible. Of the numerous Scaber Stalks, none is known to be toxic.

June–November.

RED-CRACKED BOLETE

Boletus chrysenteron   **Cap 1¼–3¼in; stalk to 2⅜in**

The dull olive-brown skin of the cap becomes cracked, showing a pink layer underneath. Pores dirty yellow to greenish. Flesh yellow, sometimes turning blue or green on bruising.

A medium-sized bolete, with stalk not swollen, and slightly bent towards the foot. Edible. The **Yellow-cracked Bolete** (*X. subtomentosus*) (**1**) has a velvety pale buff to olive-brown cap, showing yellow in the cracks. Edible.

Under broadleaved trees, especially oak, and along roads and on banks. *X. subtomentosus* is also found in mixed woods. Both are widespread in North America.

Other **boletes**. No poisonous lookalikes.

June/July–Oct./Nov.; over winter in California.

CHESTNUT BOLETE

Cap 1¼–4in; stalk to 3½in   *Gyroporus castaneus*

Small bolete with rusty brown to chestnut cap, white or pale yellow pores, not changing color when bruised. Stalk same color or paler than cap, rather uneven, brittle and hollow.

The surface of the rounded fleshy cap is smooth or slightly velvety and the stalk also has a slight bloom when young. The white flesh does not change color when cut. **Edibility suspect**.

Under broadleaved trees, especially oak and beech. Maine to Florida west to the Great Lakes and Texas. Also on the West Coast.

Bluing Bolete; other **boletes**.

June–October.

Russula virescens   Cap 2–6in; stalk to 3⅜in

1

Brittle gills and flesh typical of a russula (also called brittlegills.) Pale green or bluish-green matt cap surface flaking and cracking to show white underneath.

White stalk and gills. Spore print cream. Edible, with a mild nutty taste. The **Variable Russula** (*R. cyanoxantha*) (**1**) is bluish-green with violet overtones, not cracking, with forked gills. Edible.

Both are widespread and common in eastern North America, associated with oak, aspen and other broadleaved trees (also found in mixed woods.)

Green Quilt Russula (*R. crustosa*:) similarly cracked cap, green with orange tones, edible, spore print darker yellow; Tacky Green Russula (*R. aeruginea*:) sticky greenish cap, not cracking, edible (also occurs under lodgepole pine.)

July–September/October.

Golden Russula (*R. flavipes*) (**1**) small, cap to 3in, bright orange-yellow, dry, matt. Stalk yellow, gills white becoming yellowish. In eastern deciduous forests. Quite common. **Edibility not known**.

Firm Russula (*R. compacta*) (**2**) reddish-orange to yellowish cap, to 7in, sticky when wet, gills white to pale yellow, bruises rusty brown, spore print white. E. North America. Edible.

Purple-bloom Russula (*R. mariae*) (**3**) purple to wine red cap, to 2in, covered with a white bloom when young, white gills, white stalk flushed red in the middle. Spore print whitish to cream. In deciduous eastern woods, and near oak in grass. Good to eat.

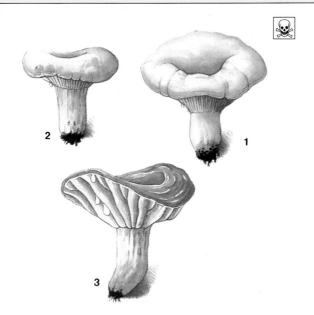

The many different Milkcaps (or Milkys) look similar to russulas but the gills release a milky fluid when broken. All have a white or very pale spore print. Many are hot and peppery to the taste, some are **toxic**, and **only a few are edible**.

Willow Milkcap) (*Lactarius controversus* (**1**) cap to 9in, dingy white, becoming vase-shaped with inrolled edge. Gills dingy pale pink. Flesh and gills release a white acrid milk which does not change color on exposure to air. Canada, Alaska, eastern USA. Under poplar and willow.

Cottonroll Milkcap (*L. deceptivus*) (**2**) cap to 10in, white, with a shaggy inrolled edge. Cream gills. Very acrid taste. White milk and brown-staining flesh. Near oak (in mixed woods near hemlock.) E. North America.

Orange Milkcap (*L. hygrophoroides*) (**3**) cap 1¼–4in, orange-brown. White gills widely spaced, like those of waxycaps. Milk copious, white, not changing color. Edible and good. In deciduous woods. E. North America.

PEPPERY MILKCAP
Cap 2–6in; stalk to 3¼in
Lactarius piperatus

1

White cap becoming sunken in center. Cream or slightly pinkish crowded gills exude a copious, very acrid milk, which stays white. White stalk does not discolor on bruising.

Cap wrinkled, gills running down the stalk slightly. The **Tawny Milkcap** (*L. volemus*) (**1**) has a pale orange, matt, wrinkled cap, crowded yellow gills and white milk that slowly turns brown. Fishy smell. A good edible.

Both are quite common in deciduous woods in eastern North America east of Great Plains (Peppery Milkcap also in Midwest.)

L. vellereus: large (to 10in) white cap with lobed edge, short stout stalk, white flesh staining yellow when cut. **No white Milkcaps are worth eating and some are toxic. Orange** and **Cottonroll Milkcaps** resemble the Tawny Milkcap.

August–November.

1

Cap pinkish to flesh-colored, with concentric paler zones. The incurved edge is very shaggy or woolly. Pinkish gills release a white unchanging acrid milk. Spore print cream.

White flesh smells faintly of geranium leaves. Stem white, pitted pink. **Poisonous**. The **Gold-drop Milkcap** (*L. chrysorrheus*) (**1**) has a smooth cap with a yellowish tinge and gills and stem bruising yellow. Edible after cooking.

L. torminosus under birch, E. North America. Almost identical species occur in the Northwest. *L. chrysorrheus* under broadleaved trees (also mixed woods), S. Canada southwards.

Saffron Milkcap; *L. thyinos*: sticky orange-ringed cap, edible; *L. rubrilacteus*: scanty reddish milk, edible; *L. peckii*: orange-zoned cap, white latex, very acrid.

August–November.

23

SWEETBREAD MUSHROOM
Cap 2–4in; stalk to 3¼in　　　*Clitopilus prunulus*

White velvety cap often becoming sunken in center, with lobed
incurved edge, and pink gills descending a white stalk. Strong
smell of bread dough. Spore print pink.

The lobed edge to cap is more marked in older specimens. Gills
are cream at first. The thick white stalk is sometimes placed off-
center. A good edible fungus but **may be confused with several
poisonous species** (see below.)

Widely distributed in North America in open woods.

Sweating Mushroom; Lead Poisoner; *Entoloma abortivum*:
cucumber-like smell, often appears with bumpy rounded masses
representing aborted fruitbodies; **Agaricus** spp, ring on stalk,
gills free; **Pink Calocybe**.

July–September, November in Southwest.

Vivid violet throughout when young, fading bluish or whitish with age. Gills thick, far apart, adnate to decurrent. Spore print white.

The cap has a matt surface covered with fine scales and soon flattens out. Stem fibrous, usually curved. Harmless but not worth eating.

In damp places and in deep leaf litter in deciduous forests. Throughout eastern North America east of the Great Plains.

Lilac Mycena; Deceiver; *L. ochropurpurea* is larger, 2–8in, with a gray-purple cap and thick purple gills.

July–October.

SOAP-SCENTED TRICH
Cap 1¾–3¼in; stalk to 3¼in

Tricholoma saponaceum

1

Fleshy fungus with a dark gray to gray-brown cap, gills sinuate, white or pale yellow. Distinctive soapy smell. White stalk pinkish at base. Spore print white.

Cap smooth, cracking into scales in dry weather. **Inedible.** The **Poplar Trich** (*T. populinum*) (**1**) has a sticky beige to reddish-brown cap (2–6in), with radial fibers. Mealy smell. Edible but easily confused with toxic trichs, **so avoid**.

Widespread throughout North America, in deciduous broadleaved woods, singly or in small groups, *T. populinum* only under cottonwoods and other poplars, on sandy soil, in clusters.

Dirty Trich; **Sticky Gray Trich**; sinuate gills and white spores distinguish trichs from similar fungi. There are several poisonous species, including some with reddish-brown caps. Some have caps streaked with radial fibers.

July–November.

PUNGENT FIBER HEAD

Inocybe sororia **Cap 1–3in; stalk to 4in**

Conical to bell-shaped cap, pale yellowish, dry and silky, with radial fibers. Strong smell of unripe corn. Spore print brown.

Poisonous. Gills whitish, with white-fringed edges (use a hand lens.) The cap often flattens out and splits at the edge, but retains the central knob. Stalk whitish, silky and solid. May grow much larger in favorable years in Northwest.

Widespread throughout North America, especially common in the Pacific Northwest. Associated with hardwoods in mixed woods, growing singly or in scattered groups.

White Fiber Head; *I. fastigiata* has no smell of green corn; fiber heads typically have brownish caps with radial fibers, brown spores, and some have a fine veil joining young cap edge to stalk, leaving a faint ring.

August–December.

Tall mushroom with tough slender stalk ending in a long underground "taproot" eventually contacting wood. Sticky yellowish-brown cap, gills pure white.

The cap often has wrinkles radiating out from center, and thin pale flesh. Gills are thick, spaced far apart, and adnexed. Stem white to brownish, fibrous and twisted. Spore print white.

Throughout eastern North America and Midwest, especially around beech (sometimes on stumps.)

The rarer *O. longipes* has a dry, slightly hairy, brownish cap, no taproot, and long, twisted stalk covered in velvety brown hairs.

July–October, November in Texas.

Sticky slimy purple cap becomes yellowish at center. Gills purplish becoming rust-colored. Stalk pale violet. Spore print rusty brown.

The stalk is also slimy and sticky to the touch. There is a violet cobwebby veil on young specimens, which soon disappears leaving no ring. Edible but not of high quality.

Throughout eastern North America in lowland deciduous woods, reported in the Northwest.

The form *C. heliotropicus* has cap streaked and spotted with yellow; *C. iodeoides* also has a slimy purplish cap, with a bitter taste. Other purple corts, such as the rare *C. violaceus* in coniferous forests, have dry or scaly caps.

August–September.

29

1

Tall white ringless stem, the base enclosed in a white sac-like volva. Dull fawn or grayish cap has a striated edge and patches of white veil remnants. Gills and spores white.

This is edible after cooking to destroy toxins, but is thin-fleshed. The **Tawny Grisette** (*A. fulva*) (**1**) is similar, but with a bright fawn cap and cream gills. Also edible after cooking. **Do not confuse with the deadly poisonous amanitas**.

Both are found in open woods and are widespread throughout North America.

A. batterae: close-fitting volva, yellowish-gray cap and stalk, rare, under conifers; the deadly **amanitas**: ring and sac-like volva or volva remnants at base of stalk; **Agaricus** spp: brown spores, ring, no volva.

June/July–Sept; Nov–Feb or (**1**) Jan–March (Calif.)

YELLOW PATCHES

Amanita flavoconia   **Cap 1–3in; stalk to 4in**

The sticky orange to yellow cap has yellowish patches, remnants of the veil. Hanging whitish ring on white or pale yellow stalk. Gills whitish. Spore print white.

The stalk bears the remains of the universal veil at the base as crumbling yellow patches. Patches on cap are often lost.

Throughout eastern North America, in oak and birch woods (also near conifers.)

American Caesar's Mushroom; Fly Agaric.

June–November.

Smooth to greasy bright orange-red cap, occasionally bearing a fragment of the white universal veil. Stalk, gills and ring yellow. White sac-like volva at base of stem.

Flesh is yellow near surface. Spore print white. Edible, but take care not to confuse it with the **Fly Agaric**.

Dry woods, especially of oak and pine, sometimes growing in fairy rings. From Quebec to Florida, and Midwest, also New Mexico and Arizona.

The **Fly Agaric** has white patches on cap; **Yellow Patches**.

July–October.

Smooth greenish-yellow to olive cap, sometimes almost white, sometimes bearing remnants of white veil. Gills white. Stalk bears a ring and large white volva. White spores.

This handsome mushroom is **deadly poisonous**, even in tiny amounts. It has a sweet smell rapidly becoming sickly. The young fruitbodies or "eggs" are completely enclosed in a universal white veil. Stalk pale, flushed same color as cap.

Widespread and locally common. Under broadleaved trees, especially oaks and liveoaks, also under conifers. Northeastern USA to Virginia, west to Ohio, and on West Coast.

Other amanitas. All the deadly amanitas have white spores, white gills, and bear both ring and volva. Wash your hands thoroughly after handling any of them.

September–November (NE,) November–January (W.)

DESTROYING ANGEL
Cap 2–5in; stalk to 8in
Amanita virosa

1

A shining pure white mushroom, occasionally with a pink tinge to cap, with a flaring fragile ring and large volva at base of stalk. White, crowded gills. White spore print.

The slightly greasy cap and scaly stalk distinguish this **deadly poisonous** amanita from the **equally deadly** all-white **Fool's Mushroom** (*A. verna*) (**1**) with a faint greenish tinge to the center of cap.

Both are found in broadleaved forests (also in coniferous forests), throughout North America.

Death Cap (white form;) there are a few more deadly all-white amanitas, such as *A. ocreata* in the Pacific Northwest which becomes buff with age, so **avoid eating any all-white mushroom, and never even taste any with a volva.**

June–November.

Oval cap with a surface like a honeycomb, not separable from stalk at lower edge. Light yellowish-brown. Stalk whitish, soon becoming hollow.

One of the best-known and most delicious edible fungi. **It should, however, be eaten with caution as it disagrees with some people**. Late in the season much larger specimens can be found, up to 12in high.

Associated with many types of broadleaved trees, old orchards and burned ground. Throughout North America.

The Black Morel (*M. elata*) has a black-ribbed conical head. It is also edible although **can cause gastric upsets if eaten with alcohol**. Appears in April–May. **False Morel; Fluted White Helvella; Half-free Morel; Wrinkled Thimble-cap**.

Late April–June, March–May (W.)

HALF-FREE MOREL
Cap ⅜–1⅝in high; stalk to 4in *Morchella semilibera*

1

Yellow-brown cap with a surface like a honeycomb and the lower edge free from stalk. Whitish hollow stalk.

Edible, appearing a week or so before the Yellow Morel. The **Wrinkled Thimble-cap** (*Verpa bohemica*) (**1**) has a wrinkled, not honeycombed, cap, attached to stalk only at the top. **Best avoided as it can cause cumulative poisoning in some people.**

In damp woods, associated with broadleaved trees. *M. semilibera* is found in the Pacific Northwest, and E. North America to Iowa, *V. bohemica* is widespread.

Yellow Morel and other morels; *V. conica* (Smooth Thimble-cap) has a smooth brownish cap like a thimble on a white stalk, and is one of the first mushrooms to be seen in the spring in the North.

April–May; (**1**) late March–May.

36

Reddish or orange-brown slimy cap with tiny yellow pores on underside, and a purplish ring on stalk.

The stalk is often covered with brownish granules above the ring, becoming white or brown below. The thick flesh is pale yellow and does not change color when bruised. Good to eat if the slime is removed first.

Common and widespread in E. North America, especially under Scots Pine, Red Pine and spruces.

The numerous *Suillus* spp. are associated with conifers, mostly have slimy caps and small yellow pores, but *S. pictus* has a scaly reddish cap, no ring, with Eastern White Pine, edible. All are edible if the slime is first removed.

September–December.

Orange-red slightly sticky conical cap. Gills nearly free, white to pale yellow. Yellowish stalk thick and slightly twisted. All parts bruise black. Spore print white.

Although this mushroom is sometimes eaten it may be poisonous and hallucinogenic **and so is best avoided**. The gills and cap have a somewhat "waxy" appearance.

In coniferous woods throughout North America, growing singly or in scattered groups.

There are many other small red or yellowish waxycaps such as the **Parrot Mushroom**; **Fading Scarlet Waxycap**; *H. coccineus*: blood-red cap and reddish gills; *Hygrophorus speciosus*: slimy orange-red cap, white gills, under larch.

July–September; November–April (Calif.)

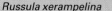

Brittle flesh and gills. Cap pinkish, blackish in center. Gills pale cream, becoming russet. Flesh turns yellow when cut and smells of crab.

The very variably colored cap pales toward the edge, becoming pink or carmine. Cap becomes sunken in center when mature. Stalk pale, yellowing toward the base. Spore print cream to ochre. Edible.

Under conifers, especially hemlock, widespread in North America.

R. krombholzii: reddish cap, sticky when wet, cream gills, white stalk, no smell of shellfish, in mixed and deciduous woods; **Fragile Russula**.

July–September.

Rosy Russula (*R. rosacea* (**1**) cap sticky, rose-red, 1–4in gills pale yellow, stalk rose-red. Peppery taste. Under conifers, especially pine, in the Rocky Mountains and Pacific Coast of North America, in fall. **Do not eat**.

Sand Russula (*R. ventricosipes*) (**2**) hard rounded yellow to brown cap with a sticky surface, 3¾–5½in. Short stalk is streaked with red. Gills pale yellow becoming edged with red.

Spore print pale orange-yellow. In sandy soil, often under pines, in Midwest and southeastern USA, late summer to fall.

Western Russula (*R. occidentalis* (**3**) light bluish-purple cap with a yellowish or greenish center, 2–5in. Gills pale yellow, stalk white, bruising reddish then black. Edible. Under conifers especially in damp places.

Lactarius deliciosus   **Cap 2–5½in; stalk to 2¾in**

Cap with concentric orange rings on a paler ground, turning green on bruising. Orange gills. Flesh and gills release a sweet orange milk with a slightly peppery aftertaste.

A large thickset fungus, becoming vase-shaped with age. Cap surface slightly frosted or shining. Milk eventually turns green. Stalk pale, thick, with orange pits. Flesh off-white. Gills crowded. Spore print cream. Edible and good.

Widespread and fairly common, especially under pine, widespread throughout North America.

L. deterrimus: cap uniformly pale orange, is often considered a subspecies; *L. thyinos*: sticky stalk, milk does not stain green; *L. peckii*: white milk; **Red-juice Milkcap**.

August–October.

Pinkish-orange gills release orange milk which immediately turns blood red. Cap dull orange, frosted, with pink and orange zones. Stipe pitted reddish-orange.

A good edible mushroom with a mild taste. Flesh white, rapidly reddening when cut. Spore print cream. The very acrid **Red-hot Milkcap** (*L. rufus*) (**1**) has a brick-red cap (2–4in) and stalk, abundant white milk and buff gills. **Not recommended**.

L. rubrilacteus is found with pine and with Douglas Fir from the Rocky Mountains westwards, *L. rufus* in damp conifer forests, widespread throughout North America.

Saffron Milkcap: orange milk; *L. rufulus*: white flesh, yellowish gills, under live oak in California, November–December; red-capped russulas: no milk.

August–November.

Smooth white cap with rusty pink spots. Crowded white gills, adnate or nearly free. Brittle white stalk, sometimes with reddish stripes. Pale pinkish-buff spore print.

Bitter and reported to be indigestible, **not recommended**. The cap often becomes flat with a wavy margin. Gills are sometimes buff-colored.

Eastern North America from Quebec to North Carolina, common in forests where it is often found associated with rotten or buried wood.

Cloudy Clitocybe; other collybias have reddish, brown, white or yellowish caps, tough stalks and adnate to free gills, spore print white or pinkish.

July–November.

Wrinkled yellow cap has a granular surface and remnants of veil around edge. Stalk is covered in granules up to the ring. Disagreeable smell. Spore print white.

Gills adnate, white to cream. The **Brownish Chroogomphus** (*Chroogomphus rutilus*) (**1**) has a sticky red-brown cap with a central "spike," small ring on stalk, brownish gills and gray to black spore print.

Widespread under conifers, growing on moss, soil or needles, *Chroogomphus rutilus* especially under pines.

Another subspecies of *C. amianthinum* has a smooth cap and no smell. *Chroogomphus* spp. all have typical peg-like caps, e.g. *C. tomentosus*, orange-yellow cap, in the west, and *C. vinicolor*, slimy wine-purple cap, widespread.

Both Aug–Oct (E&N,) Nov–Jan & (**1**) Dec–Jan (Calif.)

1

A rusty brown convoluted cap like a brain gives this fungus its alternate name of Brain Mushroom. It is set on a short stout paler, hollow stalk.

Deadly when raw and should be avoided, although eaten in some countries after long preparation. The edible **Eastern Cauliflower Mushroom** (*Sparassis crispa*) (**1**) has pale beige flat, curled, divisions.

G. esculenta is most common in the north and in mountains, *S. crispa* in eastern oak, and oak and pine, woods.

Most other False Morels are **toxic**. The larger *G. gigas*, under conifers near melting snowbanks in W. mts. is edible. The **Western Cauliflower Mushroom** (*S. radicata*) is very like *S. crispa* but has a long root, edible; **Bear's Head Tooth**.

April–June; (**1**) July–October.

1

Golden-yellow to apricot throughout, smelling faintly of apricots. The top-shaped cap soon becomes funnel-shaped, and has thick forking ridges on underside instead of true gills.

A delicious edible fungus, often found growing in troops. The small **Funnel Chanterelle** (*C. tubaeformis*) (**1**) has a yellow stalk and yellow or grayish ridges on underside of cap, which is gray-brown or yellow on top. **Not recommended for eating.**

Chanterelles are quite common in woods, especially oak (and also under conifers) throughout N. America. *C. tubaeformis* is found on moss and in damp places, in northern N. America.

The **poisonous** *Gomphus floccosus* has a scaly yellow cap, and a network of ridges on the underside looking rather like pores. **False Chanterelle**: gills, harmless; **Jack o' Lantern**: on wood, gills, **poisonous.**

June–Sept (E,) Sept–Nov (NW,) Nov–Feb (Calif.:) (**1**) July–Oct.

Fleshy lobed cap pale fawn or orange-tinged, dark russet in one form, with cream to russet teeth on underside instead of gills. Stalk white, with faint bloom, often misshapen.

A good edible fungus with a nutty taste after cooking to remove bitterness. Teeth are brittle, crowded, and run down the stalk a little way. The flesh smells faintly of orange-flower water.

Widespread throughout North America under broadleaved trees and conifers.

The Scaly Tooth (*Hydnum imbricatum*) has a brown scaly cap and teeth; **Bear's Head Tooth**.

August–November.

Date-brown fleshy cap with a greasy surface and white edge. Pores pale, slowly becoming greenish-yellow. Upper stalk covered with faint network of white.

One of the best-known edible fungi, the most delicious of the boletes, retaining its flavor on drying. The stalk is pale, streaked reddish-brown in places. The pores sometimes bruise brown.

Throughout North America under broadleaved trees (birch and aspen) and conifers (pine and hemlock.)

Other boletes and scaber stalks. Avoid boletes with pale caps, or red pores, or flesh that turns blue, as **some are toxic**.

June–October.

1

Cap rich bright brown, sticky when young or wet, small pores cream to lemon, bruising greenish-blue when mature. Stalk cylindrical rather than swollen at base.

Stalk pale brown streaked with reddish-brown. Pale flesh of cap bruises wine-red. Edible and good. The **Red-capped Scaber Stalk** (*Leccinum aurantiacum*) (**1**) is large and fleshy, with orange-brown cap, pale pores, scaly stalk. Edible and good.

B. badius is found under conifers and broadleaved trees, in association with rotten wood, in NE N. America south to N. Carolina. *L. aurantiacum* is found throughout N. America.

Other boletes and scaber stalks. Avoid boletes with pale caps, or red pores or those whose flesh turns blue, some of which are **toxic**. The scaly stalk distinguishes scaber stalks, none of which is thought to be toxic.

June–November; (**1**) August–September.

White to pale ochre cap is smooth and velvety becoming scaly. Pores white to pale ochre, turning blue when bruised. Flesh turns instantly blue when broken.

An excellent edible bolete despite the bluing flesh. Stalk is white at top, brownish from the base up to an indistinct ring-like zone which soon disappears, and becomes hollow at maturity.

In many sorts of woods, depending on area, E. North America from Canada to Florida, west to Minnesota.

Chestnut Bolete: possibly toxic.

July–September.

Large bolete, with dry gray-brown cap and thick stalk, covered in a darker network. White pores becoming salmon-pink when older.

The very bitter flesh makes this bolete **inedible**, although not toxic, and it can spoil a dish of ceps if even one is included by mistake.

In association with both broadleaved and coniferous trees, sometimes found on rotting hemlock logs, in E. USA from Maine to Florida and west to Michigan and Texas.

Other boletes.

June–November.

51

Cap covered with thick gray-brown to black scales, resembling an immature pine cone when young. Stalk with a shaggy ring, becoming indistinct in older specimens. Spores purple-brown.

This unusual bolete has whitish pores covered with a veil when young, later becoming grayish. Flesh reddens on bruising. **Inedible.**

In E. North America from Nova Scotia to Florida, west to Michigan and Texas, under oaks and in mixed deciduous/coniferous forests.

Unlikely to be confused with any other bolete.

July–October.

Tiny bell-shaped orange cap, furrowed from center to edge. Thin wiry stalk varying from white to black. Gills attached or free, pale yellow. Spore print white.

This is one of several similar tiny *Marasmius* spp. which look like small umbrellas. They typically have tough stalks and tough flesh which dries out quickly but rapidly rcvives after rain.

Found on the East Coast, on fallen leaves, pine needles and on dead and fallen wood.

M. rotula has a white umbrella-like cap and a tough shiny black stalk, grows thickly clustered on rotting wood throughout North America.

July–October.

LILAC MYCENA

Cap 1–2in; stalk to 4in   *Mycena pura*

Small fleshy rose-pink to lilac mushroom with white to pinkish gills. Smells of radishes. Fibrous stalk.

One of the more robust mycenas, the bell-shaped cap has a central knob and a striated edge. Gills adnate, quite far apart with short gills in between. Spore print white. **Not recommended** as it contains traces of the toxin muscarine.

Across northern North America and in East, Texas and Colorado, in woods of all kinds.

Mycenas have small fragile bell-shaped caps in various colors, tough stalks, adnexed or adnate to sinuate gills, white or pinkish spore prints, and apart from this one, they grow on wood; **Amethyst Tallowgill**: thick violet gills.

July–Sept (E,) Nov (Texas,) fall–spring (Calif.)

Small colorful (yellow, red, orange, pink) mushrooms which grow in moss, damp places in woods, or in some cases on rotting moss-covered logs. Appear in late summer and fall. All have rather thick "waxy" gills and white spores.

Parrot Mushroom (*Hygrophorus psittacinus*) (**1**) cap ⅜–¼in, sticky, shades of brownish-yellow-tinged greenish and/or reddish. Stalk tough, slimy, green at apex (except when old.) Gills adnate, yellowish. Heaths, pastures, grassy woods.

Fading Scarlet Waxycap (*H. miniatus*) (**2**): cap ¾–1⅝in, scarlet or orange-red, dry, with small scales in center. Gills adnate, decurrent, orange with yellow edges. On moss, rotting logs, etc. *H. coccineus* has a blood-red bell–shaped cap, yellow gills, on ground in woods.

Chanterelle Waxycap (*H. cantharellus*) (**3**): cap ⅜–1⅜in, orange-red. Gills orange-red, decurrent. Stalk dry, same color as cap or paler, base whitish. On moss, also on decaying logs.

WHITE FIBER HEAD

Cap ⅝–1¼in; stalk to 2in *Inocybe geophylla*

Cap and stalk white and silky, stalk powdery at apex only. Gills crowded, yellowish to clay brown, adnexed. Spore print brown.

One of a number of **very poisonous** small white mushrooms. Cap color can vary from white to lilac with a pale ochre tinge in center. Very young caps have the edge joined to stalk by a cobwebby veil which leaves no trace.

Widespread throughout North America, in all kinds of woods.

Inocybes often have conical caps or flatter caps with a central knob, often radically streaked and splitting at edge. Most are some shade of brown. Gills and spores brown. **All should be avoided, many are toxic**.

July–November.

Cap olive to rusty brown, felty, sticky when wet, with inrolled rim. Gills easily separable from cap, cream to dirty yellow-brown, crowded, running down stem. Spores dull brown.

A robust fungus which could at first sight be confused with some lactarias but is not milky. Gills spotted rust brown. Stalk pale brown, thick and smooth. **Not to be eaten** as it can have a cumulative toxic effect.

Widespread throughout North America, in mixed woods, sometimes on rotting wood.

P. atrotomentosus: velvety black stalk, on conifer stumps; *Gomphidius glutinosus*: sticky gray-brown cap, whitish stalk with a constriction and ring-like zone immediately beneath gills, under conifers, spore print black.

July–November.

EMETIC RUSSULA
Cap 1–3in; stalk to 4in *Russula emetica*

Brittle gills and flesh, pure scarlet or cherry-red shiny cap, white gills and stalk. Skin of cap peels completely to show white or faintly reddish flesh. Very acrid taste.

One of numerous bright red-capped russulas, this can cause vomiting in the raw state and **should be avoided**. The flesh has a distinctive smell of coconut. Gills adnate, quite widely spaced. Spore print white to yellowish.

Throughout North America in sphagnum bogs, and in boggy places in coniferous or mixed woods.

The red-capped, white-spored russulas are difficult to distinguish from each other and are all best avoided. Some red-capped russulas have cream gills, ochre to yellow spore print and a mild taste. **None is worth eating**.

August–September.

1

Brittle gills and flesh. Whitish to gray-brown cap and stalk turn black with age. Flesh reddens before blackening on cutting. Gills whitish, also bruising red then black.

Gills are usually close together. Spores white. **Inedible**. The **Stinking Russula** (*R. fragrantissima*) (**1**) has a dirty yellow-gray slimy cap, 3½–8in, and a sickening smell. Gills dirty white, spores pale cream. **Inedible**.

Throughout North America in woods of all kinds.

R. densifolia has crowded gills but otherwise is virtually identical to *R. dissimulans*; *R. nigricans*, Pacific NW, is similar but has gills spaced far apart. *R. laurocerasi* somewhat resembles *R. fragrantissima* but smells of marzipan.

July–Sept (E,) Oct–Dec NW;) (**1**) Aug–Nov.

SHORT-STALKED WHITE RUSSULA
Cap 4–8in; stalk to 3in *Russula brevipes*

1

Large white cap, with a dull dry surface. Gills and short stalk white. All parts bruise brownish. Spore print pale cream.

A large squat mushroom, with crowded gills. **Inedible**. The **Fragile Russula** (*R. fragilis*) (**1**) has a sticky reddish cap (1–3in,) but sometimes orange, yellowish or greenish. Gills and stalk white. Spore print yellowish. Peppery taste.

Throughout North America in mixed woods, *R. fragilis* sometimes on rotten wood or moss.

White lactarias exude a milky juice when broken. *R. fragilis* with its variably colored cap may be confused with several other russulas. It is most easily identified when several different colors are present in the same cap.

July–October; (**1**) July–September.

Flesh and gills release abundant white milk when broken. Reddish-brown wrinkled cap, sometimes sunken in center, with a fishy smell.

Cap edge often much wrinkled. Gills buff-colored, crowded. Stalk stout, reddish-brown, velvety. Spore print white. Edible and good.

In deciduous and mixed woods in eastern North America.

Tawny Milkcap; Orange Milkcap.

June–September.

AROMATIC MILKCAP
Cap ⅝–2in; stalk to 2¼in   *Lactarius camphoratus*

Dark chestnut-brown cap, fading to reddish. Strong smell of "wet linen" when fresh. Flesh and gills release a watery milk. Gills reddish-brown. Spore print cream.

A small slender lactarius. When dried the flesh has a strong spicy smell resembling curry powder and can be used as a seasoning. The cap often becomes funnel-shaped but retains a small central knob.

In coniferous and mixed forests, throughout northeastern North America.

Red-hot Milkcap: Larger, acrid milk, no scent; *L. rufulus:* in California, yellowish gills, no scent.

August–October.

Blue cap, stalk and gills, releasing a little dark-blue milk when broken.

Almost unmistakable because of its unusual color when young, but fading with age. The white flesh turns blue then green when cut. The milk also eventually turns dark green on exposure to air. Edible.

In oak and pine woods, eastern North America west to Michigan and Texas.

L. uvidus has a dull lilac cap and white milk staining the flesh violet; *L. paradoxus* has a sticky silvery cap, purple-brown milk.

July–October.

Fleshy cap convex, becoming flatter with central hump. Yellowish-gray cap and stalk. Gills thin, crowded, cream to yellowish, slightly decurrent. Spore print white.

Do not eat as it disagrees with some people and can be confused with toxic species. The **Fat-footed Clitocybe** (*C. clavipes*) (**1**) has a club-shaped downy base to stalk, and watery flesh smelling of bitter almonds. Not worth eating.

C. nebularis is confined to the Rocky Mountains and West Coast in mixed and coniferous woods, *C. clavipes* is widespread throughout North America.

There are numerous other clitocybes in North America, e.g. **Sweating Mushroom**, **Blewit**. They are fleshy, white-spored mushrooms, with decurrent to adnate gills and white, brown, violet or grayish caps.

Aug–Dec, over winter (Calif.;) (**1**) July–Nov, Dec–Feb (Calif.)

Entoloma sinuatum (lividum)

One of the larger entolomas. Creamy yellow to pale coffee-colored, slippery cap. Gills adnexed, almost free, not crowded, yellowish, turning pink. Silky stalk. Spores pink.

Large fleshy fungus with cap edge incurved in young specimens becoming wavy-edged when old. The thick white firm flesh smells slightly of cucumber or new-ground meal. **Highly poisonous**, causing cramps, severe vomiting and diarrhea.

Widespread throughout North America, under broadleaved trees (also under conifers,) singly or in groups.

Cloudy Clitocybe; Pink Calocybe; Sweetbread Mushroom (decurrent gills;) other entolomas (sinuate or adnexed gills, pink spores;) **tricholomas** (sinuate gills, white spores.)

July–November.

Distinctive large smooth bluish-lilac cap when young, becoming tan. Gills sinuate, lilac becoming yellowish, and can be separated easily from cap. Spore print pinkish-buff.

This pleasant-smelling mushroom is good to eat after cooking (although some people are allergic to it) but is slightly toxic when raw. Stalk stout, fibrous, lilac. The flesh is thick, firm and white with a lilac tinge.

Widespread throughout North America in open woods, along paths, in gardens, often growing in groups.

L. saeva has no smell, a buff cap, pinkish-beige gills, lilac stalk, in grass and wood edges, edible. Make sure you do not have **Lead Poisoner** which also has a pinkish spore print, or a **tricholoma** (white spores.)

August–December, November–March (Calif.)

Hebeloma crustuliniforme

Slimy cream to russet cap with paler margin. Gills crowded, pale brownish-gray to cinnamon-brown, edged with water droplets when young. Spore print brown to rust.

Poisonous. This mushroom smells of radishes when young, has a bitter taste and **can cause severe gastric upsets**. The stout cylindrical stalk is white, flaky, with white granules on surface toward apex.

In association with both coniferous and broadleaved trees, sometimes forming fairy rings, often in suburban areas, widespread in North America but most common in west.

The well-named Corpse Finder (*H. syriense*) has a sticky red-brown cap with whitish gills and has often been found to mark the site of a buried body. Hebelomas typically have slimy caps, fringed edges to the gills and brown spores.

September–November, through May in California.

Sticky Gray Trich (*Tricholoma portentosum*) (**1**) cap 2–5in, gray-brown, slightly conical, tinged yellowish, with dark fibrils radiating out from blackish center. Sinuate gills and stalk white, tinged lemon. Spore print white. An excellent edible mushroom with a floury smell. Widespread.

Canary Trich or **Cavalier** (*T. flavovirens*) (**2**) has a sticky yellow cap (2–4in,) nearly free yellow gills, and white spores. Found under pine in sandy soils, throughout North America.

Edible, but do not confuse with *T. sulphureum* (all parts sulfur yellow, smells of coal tar) or *T. sejunctum* (blackish radial fibrils on cap,) which are **toxic**.

Dirty Trich (*T. pardinum*) (**3**) cap 2–6in, large mushroom with a fleshy cap incurved at edges, covered with brownish scales on a paler ground. Stout smooth pale stem. Gills whitish. Earthy smell becoming unpleasant. Spore print white. **Highly poisonous**. Under conifers in mixed woods in northern North America.

Dark orange fungus, cap soon sunken in center. Gills forked, bright orange, running down stalk. No distinctive smell. Spore print white to cream.

This Chanterelle lookalike is sometimes considered edible but is **not recommended**. The surface of the cap is matt, dry and sometimes downy, and eventually becomes brownish. The flesh is yellowish and rather tough.

Widespread throughout North America, under conifers or on decayed conifer wood.

Chanterelle; Jack o'Lantern: poisonous, grows on wood.

August–November, over winters in California.

Large fleshy mushroom with reddish-brown cap and stalk, the stalk bearing bright red irregular diagonal bands which are the remnants of a partial veil. Rust-brown spore print.

The bell-shaped cap ranges from fawn to dark russet, with a slightly silky surface. Stalk thick, pale russet with a bulbous base. Gills pale brown becoming dark rust. The white cortina leaves a whitish band on upper stalk. Edible.

Often near birch, common, in mixed woods. Northern North America, from Quebec to New Jersey, and west to Idaho.

Species of **Cortinarius** have variously colored caps and all have rust-brown spores. Gills adnate or sinuate. They should be identified with care as **some are deadly**, e.g. the tawny-capped and orange-veiled *C. gentilis*, under conifers.

August–October.

Cortinarius semisanguineus

Reddish-brown ring-like remnants of veil on stalk. Cap velvety, pale yellowish- to olive-brown, with a central knob. Blood-red crowded adnate gills. Spore print brown.

One of several corts with red gills. Edge of cap attached to stalk by a fine veil when young. Stalk yellowish. Flesh pale, yellowish, smelling faintly of radishes. Not edible and **may be toxic**.

Quite common and widespread throughout northern North America, especially the Pacific Northwest, associated with deciduous and coniferous trees, often in moss.

C. sanguineus: blood-red cap, gills, stalk, with conifers;
C. cinnabarinus: more orange-red, especially under oak and beech, eastern; *C. orellanus*: **deadly**, orange to rusty brown gills, orange-brown cap, high in Rocky Mts. and NW.

July–November.

GREEN STROPHARIA
Cap 1–3in; stalk to 3in   *Stropharia aeruginosa*

Slimy cap is a bright bluish-green when young, becoming yellowish with age, and has white fleecy scales at the edge. The stalk has a grayish ring. Gills adnate, violet-gray.

The slimy stalk is smooth above the ring, fleecy or covered with white flecks below, and paler than the cap. The vivid color of the cap soon fades, and the gills become chocolate-brown. Spore print purplish-brown. **Inedible.**

Eastern USA south of Great Lakes, and in Pacific Northwest and Southern California, in grass and woody litter on forest floor.

S. ambigua has a yellow cap with fleecy white edge and whitish fleecy stalk, edibility unknown.

August–October.

Pale golden to dull ocher-yellow cap sometimes with silvery veil frosting center. Gills pale becoming clay-brown, edges finely toothed (under a hand lens.) Whitish ring on stalk.

Pale brown spores. Stalk pale, striated, ring fleshy and remaining on stalk for a long time. Gills adnate, thick and crowded. Very good to eat if mushrooms can be found undamaged by insects.

Eastern, northern and northwestern North America, in coniferous and deciduous forests.

Hebeloma spp: no ring or very indistinct ring-like remains of veil on stalk; **Agaricus** spp. have dark purple-brown spore print; **corts** have no persistent ring on stalk.

September–November.

"Parasol" cap smooth and brown at center, covered elsewhere with beige to whitish scales. Free gills. Stalk shaggy up to a ring zone, smooth above. Spore print white.

One of numerous small "parasol" mushrooms with scaly caps. Gills white and very soft. Fragments of the veil edge the cap in young specimens. Stalk whitish and slightly swollen towards base. **Poisonous.**

Widespread in North America, in coniferous and mixed woods, and with oak, commonest in Northwest and in mountains.

There are many species of small lepiotas, **none should be eaten**; *L. cristata*: pungent smell; *L. josserandii*, musty smell, thick stalk, small brown scales on cap, faint ring; and *L. helveola*, persistent ring, are **deadly**.

July–November, November–February (Calif.)

Unmistakable bright red cap covered with small white patches of the universal veil. White gills and spores. White stalk with ring. Volva only a series of ridges at base of stalk.

The mushroom illustrated in countless fairy tales. Young fruitbodies are entirely covered in a white veil. The white patches may become washed off in older specimens and caps fade orange-red. **Poisonous.**

In the Rocky Mountains and the West Coast, reported but rare in northeastern USA. Under pine, spruce, birch, live oak and madrone (in California.)

American Caesar's Mushroom: smooth red cap, yellow stalk and gills, large sac-like white volva; a yellow-capped variant of the Fly Agaric with buff patches is common in the East; **Yellow Patches**.

July–October, winter in California.

BLUSHER
Cap 2–6in; stalk to 8in

Amanita rubescens

Red-brown cap covered with small dingy pinkish patches of veil. Gills and spores white. Stalk white, flushed pink with hanging ring. No apparent volva. Flesh white, bruising pink.

This is one of the edible amanitas, but **must be cooked** as it is indigestible when raw. Gills are speckled pink in older specimens. Do not confuse with **The Panther**.

Eastern North America and California under oak, white pine, often found in wooded city parks.

The Panther: **deadly poisonous**, white scales on cap, basal bulb with remains of volva, flesh does not turn pink; *A. spissa*: dark brown cap with grayish scales, flesh does not turn pink, not poisonous, but not worth eating.

June–October, February–April in California.

THE PANTHER

Amanita pantherina

Cap 1–6in; stalk to 7in

1

Red-brown to coffee-colored cap dotted with white scales. Gills, stalk, and ring are pure white. Bracelet-like remains of volva girdle stalk above base.

This is **highly poisonous**. The **Jeweled Amanita** (*A. gemmata*) (**1**) has a yellow cap (1–4in) with large irregular white scales and a striated edge, white or lemon stalk, and a fragile ring that soon disappears. **Inedible**.

Both found under coniferous trees, *A. pantherina* especially under Douglas Fir, mainly from West Coast to Rocky Mountains, rare in East, *A. gemmata* throughout North America.

The Blusher; *A. spissa*: dull brown cap with grayish scales and volva in ridges around base of stalk. Although edible, **avoid** for fear of confusion with The Panther; *A citrina*: lemon cap with white scales, edge not striated.

June/July–Oct; Nov–Feb (Calif.)

FLUTED WHITE HELVELLA
Cap ⅝–2¼in; stalk to 3½in *Helvella crispa*

Whitish thin saddle-shaped cap, with wavy lobes, and with no gills, pores or ridges on underside. White stalk is deeply furrowed and hollow.

Cap is slightly hairy on the undersurface and is attached to stalk only at center. **Inedible**.

Quite common on East Coast, Colorado, Arizona, California and Pacific Northwest, in both broadleaved and conifer forests, often in open grassy glades.

H. lacunosa: blackish cap, pale ribbed stalk; *H. elastica*: smaller, with a brownish cap on slender pale stalk; **Morel**: rounded cap with honeycombed surface; *Verpa conica*: smooth brown bell-shaped cap.

July–Oct (E,) Dec–April (SW,) Sept–Oct (NW.)

Recognizable by its shape and strong offensive smell. The stout spongy white stalk carries a slimy fetid green-black mass of spores at its tip.

The slime and spores are eventually eaten by flies, exposing the pitted surface of the cap. The immature fruitbody is like an "egg," its remnants forming a volva-like sac at stalk base.

Found to the west and south of the Great Lakes, in woods.

P. ravenelii: very similar, East and Midwest, surface of cap smooth under slime; *Mutinus caninus*: smaller, spores borne direct on tip of stalk; *Dictyophora* spp: net-like skirt hangs down under spore mass, eastern USA south to Mexico.

August–November.

PIGSKIN POISON PUFFBALL
Fruitbody 1–4in across *Scleroderma citrinum*

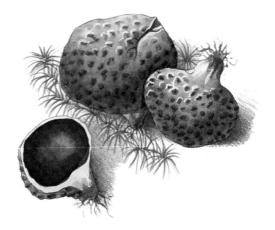

Hard ball-like fungus growing directly on the ground, with a dirty yellowish warty outer covering, becoming cracked, and a marbled purple spore mass inside.

This common earth-ball has no stalk and "roots" directly into the ground. The internal mass of spores is initially whitish, eventually turns purple and escapes through an apical pore and cracks in the hard outer wall. **Poisonous.**

Common and widespread throughout North America in woods, near trees, especially on sandy soil.

True puffballs are soft to the touch, e.g. **Gem-studded Puffball**, **Western Lawn Puffball**; **Pear-shaped Puffball**.

July-November.

80

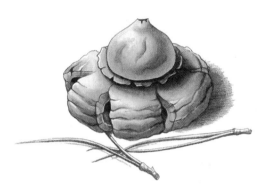

Yellowish gray-brown sac containing spores sits in a saucer supported on curved-back segments of fruitbody outer wall, which has split radially.

In this earthstar, the rays are rather fleshy and cracked across. It also has a distinct halo around the small opening in the inner sac through which the spores are released.

Throughout North America, in woods.

G. fornicatum: rays form a four- or five-legged support up to 2in high; *G. pectinatum*: spore sac has a beaked mouth; smaller; *G. saccatum*: round sac surrounded by star-like rays.

August–October.

White coral-like fruitbody, branching, with expanded toothed tips to branches. Flesh white.

One of several types of Coral Fungi. Some related species have thick unbranched club-like fruitbodies. *C. cristata* is edible, but some other species are not.

Throughout North America, on the ground in woods of all kinds, related species also occur in grass or grow directly on wood.

C. cinerea: ash-gray but otherwise very similar; *Ramaria* spp: generally more massive, lilac, yellow, pale pink or olive, not pure white.

June–October.

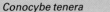

Cap conical to bell-shaped, brown, dry, with fine radial lines. Color fades with age. Gills nearly free, brown. Spore print red-brown.

Stalk straight and fragile, brown, with fine lines. One of numerous "little brown mushrooms," some of which are **deadly poisonous**. None should be eaten.

Throughout North America, in lawns and other grass, and on rich soil.

C. filiaris: movable ring on stalk, cap flattens out, off-white gills, **deadly**; **Liberty Cap**; **Lawn Mower's Mushroom**; **Mycena** spp, have white spores, *Panaeolus* spp. have black mottled gills, grow mostly on manure.

May–July, September.

LIBERTY CAP
Cap ⅜–1in; stalk to 4in *Psilocybe semilanceata*

1

Narrow pointed pale yellow-brown to tan cap with a slimy
surface, never expanding, and pale wavy stalk. Gills adnexed,
grayish becoming brown. Spore print purple-brown.

This contains the hallucinogenic drug psilocybin and **can cause
delirium**. **Mountain Moss Psilocybe** (*Ps. montana*) (**1**) is dark
brown throughout, with a striate edge to a hemispherical cap
which opens flat with a central knob.

Ps. semilanceata is common in the Pacific Northwest and is also
found elsewhere in North America, in tall grass and pastures.
Ps. montana is a western species, in mountains.

**Avoid all "little brown mushrooms" as some are deadly. Brown
Dunce's Cap; Lawn Mower's Mushroom; Psathyrella**: black
spores; *Bolbitius*: shrivels rapidly, brown spores, usually on dung;
Mycena: white spores; **Galerina**; brown spores.

August–November; (**1**) July–September.

SWEATING MUSHROOM

Clitocybe dealbata **Cap ⅜–1⅝in; stalk to 2in**

Small creamy white mushroom, with pinky-brown markings on older caps. Gills thin, adnate-decurrent, creamy, crowded. Stalk white and silky. Spore print white.

A **highly poisonous** species which could be gathered in mistake for several edible mushrooms. It contains the toxin muscarine which produces sweating, blurred vision and involuntary muscle movements.

Widespread throughout North America, common in lawns and in grass generally, including grassy glades in open woods.

Take care not to pick with the **Fairy Ring Mushroom**, near which it often grows. There are several white clitocybes, characterized by thin decurrent gills and white spores, e.g. *Clit. dilatata*: larger, in Pacific NW, **toxic**.

July–September, November–February (Calif.)

A common mushroom forming large rings in lawns and pastures. Moist, bell-shaped rusty brown cap flattens out and pales to yellowish-brown. Stalk tough, felty. Spore print white.

Gills off-white, attached or free. Like all *Marasmius* species, this tough mushroom quickly revives on moistening after drying out. Good to eat if the tough stalks are discarded.

Widespread throughout North America, very common in lawns, pastures and by paths.

Take care not to confuse with poisonous whitish clitocybes such as the **Sweating Mushroom**; **Mycena** spp. also have white spores; **Inocybes**, some of which are **poisonous**, have brown spores.

May–November.

1

Reddish-brown to pinkish-brown smooth cap sunken in center. Gills pinkish, thick, slightly waxy and spaced quite far apart. Stalk dry, pinkish-brown. Spore print white.

Often hard to identify. Gills adnate decurrent. **Inedible. Lawn Mower's Mushroom** (*Psathyrella foenisecii*) (**1**) has dull brown bell-shaped caps, ⅜–1¼in, drying paler in center. Brown gills adnate, mottled. Spores brown. **Not recommended.**

L. laccata is widespread from Canada south, on moss, in damp places, and also on poor sandy soil and wasteland. *P. foenisecii* is very common in lawns and short grass.

Amethyst Tallowgill; **Mycena** spp; **Hygrophorus** spp. have waxy gills and white spores; many other small brown psathyrella species grow in similar situations.

June–November; (**1**) May–July (both over winter in Calif.)

87

A rather stout squat mushroom, with fleshy buff to dull orange cap. The pale buff gills are waxy, widely spaced and run down and merge with stalk. Spore print white.

An excellent edible mushroom. The surface of the cap is dry and matt and often cracks around the center. The thick gills are thin-edged and have short gills interspersed between them. The stalk is stout, and a similar color to gills.

Throughout North America, singly or in clusters in meadows, lawns, grassy copses, and also in woods.

Chanterelle: ridges on underside of cap, not gills, orange-yellow; **False Chanterelle**.

May–December; November–March (Calif.)

Pink fleshy cap, flattening out but with central knob. Gills white to cream, narrow and crowded, decurrent. Spore print white.

Stalk is thick and fibrous, pinkish, hollow, and slightly hairy. **Inedible**.

Widespread but not common in lawns, grassy woodland glades, etc.

Do not confuse with toxic white clitocybes; Amethyst Tallowgill.

August–October.

FRIED-CHICKEN MUSHROOM
Cap 1–5in; stalk to 4in   *Lyophyllum decastes*

Smooth moist, shiny yellowish-gray to reddish-brown cap, crowded white adnate or decurrent gills. Stalk whitish. Spore print white.

The caps begin convex and then flatten out, and the gills become straw-colored with age. Good to eat, with a taste of fried chicken when cooked, but **take care not to confuse with toxic mushrooms** growing in similar situations.

Widespread throughout North America, in thick clusters in grassy copses, yards, parks, waste places, by roads.

Lead Poisoner and other entolomas have a pinkish spore print; **Cloudy Clitocybe**; other species of *Lyophyllum* have blackish or white caps.

June–October, over winter in California.

VELVETY PSATHYRELLA

Psathyrella velutina   Cap 2–4in; stalk to 4in

Brown to blackish gills "weep" black droplets. Gray-brown velvety or scaly cap with a woolly edge often blackened by spores. Ring-like marking from veil on stalk. Spores black.

Gills adnate, mottled, with white edges. Fibrous stalk. Edible. One of the larger psathyrellas, some others are very small and delicate. The edge of young cap is attached to stalk by a fine veil in some, but not all, psathyrellas.

Widespread throughout North America, on bare soil, beside paths, in grass.

P. candolleana: fragile, creamy-white cap, gills pale brownish-lilac, stalk white, faint ring soon vanishes, around stumps, in grass; other **psathyrellas**; **Cortinarius** spp: rusty brown spores; **Inocybe** spp: pale brown spores.

June–September.

SPRING AGROCYBE

Cap 1¼–3½in; stalk to 4in *Agrocybe praecox*

Beige-brown cap fading to dull yellow-gray. Shaggy margin to cap. Gills adnexed, crowded, whitish to dingy brown. Ring high on a slender fibrous stalk. Spore print dark brown.

Although harmless and sometimes considered edible it is not of high quality and **should be avoided** for fear of confusion with other rather nondescript poisonous mushrooms. Flesh pale, with a smell of new-ground meal.

Widespread in North America, in grassy copses and thickets, lawns, bare soil.

A. dura: cap cracking; *A. acericola*: yellow cap; **Agaricus** spp: free gills; **Hebeloma** spp: slimy caps.

April–June.

Coprinus comatus   **Cap to 6in high; stalk to 8in**

1

Shaggy white young cap eventually dissolves into an inky fluid as gills autodigest from the edge of cap inwards. Crowded whitish gills turn black from tips. Black spores.

Edible when all-white. The **Alcohol Inkcap** (*C. atramentarius*) (**1**) has a smoother cap, gray, brown-tinged at center. **Do not eat with**, or for a day or two after or before taking **alcohol**, when it causes symptoms similar to the drug Antabuse.

Both are common and widespread throughout North America, in clusters on pastures, lawns, by roadsides, paths, and on bare soil.

Many but not all *Coprinus* species have gills that turn black and dissolve. **Mica Cap**; **Agaricus** spp: gills do not dissolve; **Parasol**: gills do not dissolve.

May–June and fall, November–January (SE.)

SMOOTH VOLVARIELLA
Cap 2–6in; stalk to 8in *Volvariella speciosa*

A tall elegant mushroom whose silky white stalk has a sac-like volva at base, but no ring. Cap whitish to gray-brown. Gills pale, becoming salmon-pink. Spore print pink.

Edible but **do not confuse with young deadly amanitas** as the young mushrooms are completely enclosed in a white veil forming "eggs" like those of amanitas. The sticky cap is at first conical and then opens out. **Not recommended**.

Widespread throughout North America, in grass in broadleaved woods, on matured soil, yards, compost heaps, in pastures on rich soil.

V. bombycina: shaggy or felty cap, grows on stumps or logs, especially of elm; **amanitas**: ring as well as volva, white gills and spores; **Agaricus** spp: ring on stalk, no volva, purple-brown spore print.

June–July (N,) October–April (South and Calif.)

These delicious wild cousins of the commercial mushroom are common in pastures and other grassland in early fall. The genus *Agaricus* has white or brownish caps, a ring on stalk (but no volva,) pinkish or grayish gills often becoming black, and a dark brown spore print. Not all agarics are edible and **some are toxic. Avoid** those with an unpleasant or creosote-like smell. Only eat a small quantity the first time.

Meadow Mushroom (*Agaricus campestris*) (**1**) cap 1–4in, silky white when young. Ring narrow. Deep pink gills become brownish. *A. bitorquis*, larger, brownish cap, double-edged ring, edible, in urban areas.

A bisporus (**2**) is the wild form of the cultivated mushroom. It has a wider ring and pale fawn cap.

Horse Mushroom (*Agaricus arvensis*) (**3**) cap 3–6in, creamy, then russet. All parts bruise yellow. Gills pinkish-gray to dull brown, becoming blackish. Fleshy ring on stalk. **Do not confuse** this good edible mushroom with the **Yellow Foot Agaricus**.

YELLOW FOOT AGARICUS

Cap 2¼–7in; stalk to 6in   *Agaricus xanthodermus*

Flesh at base of stalk stains deep golden yellow when this mushroom is cut lengthways. The silky white cap also turns yellow at edges and where damaged.

This is **highly indigestible** and causes severe gastric upsets if eaten. The bright yellow flesh at the base of the stalk is the main distinguishing feature. Like all *Agaricus* species the spore print is dark purplish-brown.

Pacific Northwest south to California, in parks, yards, roadsides and under broadleaved trees in grassy places.

Several good edible mushrooms also stain yellow or become yellow with age, such as *A. silvicola*, in woods, and **Horse Mushroom**, in fields, but no other has the golden-yellow flesh at base of stalk.

September–November (NW,) November–March (Calif.)

This excellent edible mushroom has a thick double-edged ring which can be slid up and down the tall slender stalk, and a scaly parasol-shaped cap with shaggy edges. Gills cream.

The brown cap surface breaks up into a central brown patch surrounded by brownish-beige scales on a paler ground. The scaly stalk has brown zones and a slightly swollen base. The pale flesh does not redden on cutting. Spore print white.

Eastern North America from Quebec to Florida, and Midwest. In open grassy woods, and along roads (sometimes forming fairy rings.)

L. americana: edible, bruises and ages dark red, on sawdust, waste places; *L. naucina*; smooth white cap, in grass; **Shaggy Parasol**; **Green Parasol**; smaller **lepiotas**: ring is not movable, **avoid**; **Agaricus** spp: brown spore print.

July–October, November–December (Fla.)

SHAGGY PARASOL
Cap 3–8in; stalk to 8in   *Lepiota rachodes*

Pale beige cap with coarse shaggy scales, grayish, beige, light or dark brown, and a smooth central area. Thick double ring moves on smooth stalk. Gills and spore print white.

White flesh turns saffron yellow when cut or bruised. The creamy-white stalk has a swollen base and bruises brownish. Edible and good, although forms from Southern California are **reported to cause gastric upsets**.

Throughout North America, in disturbed soil, on compost heaps, along roads, sometimes forming fairy rings.

L. americana: spindle-shaped stalk, bruises and ages dark red, but young flesh is yellow when cut; **Parasol**; **Shaggy Ink Cap**; **Green Parasol**; **Agaricus** spp: dark brown spore print.

Sept.–Oct.; Nov.–Feb. (Calif.)

Green gills and spore print distinguish this **toxic** mushroom. Cap white, scaly, and buff at center. Gills white, free, becoming drab gray-green.

Smooth white stalk bears a double-edged, often movable ring. The dry hemispherical cap flattens out with age, the central scales breaking up into many small scales.

Common in the southern United States from Florida to California, including Colorado, and reported in New England, and Michigan. In lawns, pastures, etc., often in fairy rings.

Parasol; **Shaggy Parasol**; **Agaricus** spp. have dark brown spore prints.

August–September.

Club-shaped thin-walled white fruitbody is firm at first, then soft, puffing out a cloud of powdery spores if pressed. Outer surface covered with small blunt spines.

In this common puffball the spore mass becomes olive-green at maturity, and the fruitbody discolors to a dirty yellowish-brown, and loses its spines. Good to eat when still white and firm throughout.

Throughout North America, common either singly or clustered in urban parks, along roads, or in open grassy woods.

Pear-shaped Puffball: on wood; **Giant Puffball**; **Western Lawn Puffball**; *L. echinatum*: spines ¼in; *Bovista pilea*: globular, surface flakes off exposing bronze inner wall, becomes detached from ground and rolls about; **Pigskin Poison Puffball**.

July–October.

1

This enormous puffball can weigh several pounds. It has a slightly flaky white outer surface. The internal spore mass is white, becoming brown and powdery.

Good to eat when still white and firm throughout. The **Western Lawn Puffball** (*Vascellum pratense*) (**1**) is much smaller and the spore mass is delimited from the sterile spongy base by a distinct membrane. Edible when young.

C. gigantea is an eastern species, of open woods, pastures and urban parks and grass. *V. pratense* is common in grass throughout North America, especially on the Pacific west coast.

There is an almost identical western species of giant puffball, and *C. booniana* is also large with a warty surface; *Bovista pilea* becomes detached from ground and rolls about; *B. plumbea* has a bluish-gray inner wall.

May–July and fall; (**1**) September–November.

CUP FUNGI
Fruitbody 2¼–3¼in across   *Peziza vesiculosa*

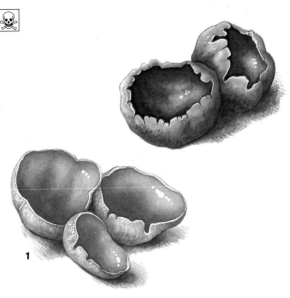

1

The pale yellow-brown fruitbody is at first round, becoming cup-shaped with an incurved edge. The inner surface (which bears the spores,) is yellowish and blistered in center.

It is best not to eat this or similar fungi. Although some are edible after cooking, others are **highly poisonous**. The cups of **Orange Peel** (*Aleuria aurantia*) (**1**) are 1–4in across, and downy on the paler outer surface. Edible.

Both occur throughout North America, *P. vesiculosa* on manure heaps and manured soil, *A. aurantia* in clusters along roadsides, in new lawns and on disturbed soil.

There are many types of cup fungi: with scarlet, pink, bright yellow, brown, or black fruitbodies. Cup-shaped jelly fungi have a more gelatinous consistency. Bird's Nest Fungi (e.g. **Splash Cups**) have cups containing tiny round "eggs."

June–Oct., Nov.–Feb. (W. Coast;) (**1**) May–Oct.

The brittle, coral-like fruitbody bears many tufts of hanging pointed teeth ¼–¾in long. Creamy to ivory white at first, becoming tough and pinkish with age.

This striking fungus is edible when young. The flesh is brittle and white, but becomes tough in older specimens, although the spines themselves often remain edible and good.

Northeastern North America to N. Carolina and west to Minnesota, on logs and stumps and on wounds on living broadleaved trees, especially beech, hickory, maple and oak.

H. abietis: larger, pinkish-buff with age, Pacific NW;
H. erinaceus: spines ¾–1¾in long, on living deciduous trees;
H. ramosum: whitish toothed mass, more irregular in appearance, along dead branches. All edible when young.

August–October.

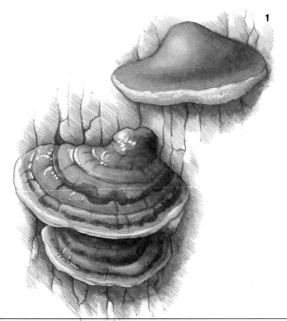

Growing as a series of "brackets," the hard gray-brown bumpy upper surface becomes covered in a layer of rusty spores from the cap above. White undersurface turns brown when scratched.

The upper surface is shiny before it becomes dusty with spores. The **Birch Polypore** (*Piptoporus betulinus*) (**1**) (to 10in across) has a smooth matt grayish-brown upper surface, and white pores and flesh on underside. Spores white.

G. applanatum occurs throughout N. America, on dead trunks of broadleaved trees. *P. betulinus* is found south to N. Carolina and in the Midwest, on both living and dead birches.

G. lucidum and *G. tsugae*: shiny reddish top, often stalked, on deciduous and coniferous trees respectively; **Red-belted Polypore**; *Daedalea quercina*: gray-brown top, brown below, pore surface like a maze.

All year round.

BEEFSTEAK POLYPORE

Fistulina hepatica   **Cap to 10in across**

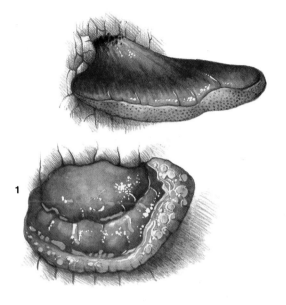

The cut flesh of this reddish-brown leathery shelf-fungus yields a red juice, and looks and feels like red meat. Yellowish tubes on underside.

Although edible after boiling, it does not live up to its name. **The Red-belted Polypore** (*Fomitopsis pinicola*) (**1**) is a hard-topped often hoof-shaped bracket, dark reddish-brown above, usually red at edge, and white below.

F. hepatica: chiefly in NE USA, on dead oaks or at base of trees. *Fomitopsis pinicola*: on many types of wood, south to N Carolina in east, also California, Arizona and Ohio.

Fom. officinalis: on conifers, hoof-shaped bracket, white to yellowish above, white pores; *Phellinus igniarius*: hard cracked upper surface is gray to black with a velvety margin, underside yellow to brown-gray, on deciduous trees.

July–October; (**1**) all year.

Circular to kidney-shaped polypore with a short thick lateral stalk and a soft leathery surface breaking up into rings of pale to dark brown scales on a yellowish ground. White pores.

This is edible when very young and tender, but soon becomes tough. The white flesh has a faint smell of honey. The white to yellowish pores run some way down the stalk.

Eastern North America to North Carolina, and Midwest, on dead and living broadleaved trees.

This is just one of many *Polyporus* spp. and relatives. They have soft leathery tops in contrast to the hard bracket-fungi. The edible Hen of the Woods (*Grifola frondosa*) has large clusters of gray-brown fleshy spoon-shaped caps.

May–November.

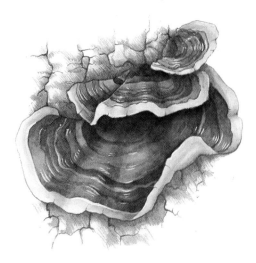

Thin silky-topped leathery brackets are concentrically zoned in shades of olive, purple, green, gray and black. Underside whitish.

Logs are sometimes smothered in the brackets of this common species. The color zones alternate velvety and smooth. One of many small thin bracket-fungi, some known as Parchment Fungi, that attack dead wood or cause disease in living trees.

Common throughout North America on dead wood of all kinds, also in wounds on living trees.

T. hirsuta: top white and felty; *T. velutina*: thicker, pores grayish; *Trichaptum biformis*: velvety grayish top, violet at edge, pores break into teeth; *Stereum ostrea*: small fan-shaped bracket, hairy cap with shiny brown zones, buff pores.

May–December.

OYSTER MUSHROOM
Cap 2–8in across   *Pleurotus ostreatus*

Fleshy semicircular or shell-shaped caps growing directly out of wood or attached with a very short (¼in) stalk. Upper surface brownish or bluish-gray fading to brown. White gills.

A good edible fungus when young, with firm white flesh and a pleasant smell. Cap has a waxy sheen when young and color can vary from white to dark gray-brown. Gills decurrent. Spore print white to lilac.

Throughout North America, common on dead trunks and branches, especially of broadleaved trees. Can also attack living broadleaved trees, and more rarely, conifers.

Pleurocybella porrigens: wavy-edged, broad, thin, white stalkless caps, white gills, on conifers; *P. dryinus*: white scaly cap, cylindrical stalk; *Panellus serotinus*: sticky yellowish cap, yellowish gills, stubby stalk, on dead wood.

All year round.

VELVET FOOT

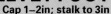

Flammulina velutipes   **Cap 1–2in; stalk to 3in** ↑

1

Clusters of flat, sticky, honey-colored to bright red-brown caps on dark brown velvety stalks. Gills yellowish, adnexed. Spore print white.

Edible after the slimy skin is removed but not of high quality. **Sulfur Tuft** (*Naematoloma fasciculare*) (**1**), has a yellow cap (1–3¼in,) sulfur-yellow gills turning black-brown, yellow stalk and brown spore print. **Toxic**.

Both are found throughout North America, growing in clusters on stumps and logs of broadleaved trees, *N. fasciculare* also on the ground in association with buried wood.

N. capnoides: cap more orange, gills grayish-brown, on coniferous wood; *N. sublateritium*: pinkish-red cap, grayish gills, on deciduous wood; **Honey Mushroom**.

Oct-May, July-Aug (mts;) (**1**) spring, fall, over winter (Calif.)

Conical pale gray-brown cap flattens out on aging. Gills pale, grayish, sometimes tinged pinkish. Stalk tough, smooth, same color as cap, "rootlike" at base. Spore print white.

Less fragile than some other mycenas. **Inedible. Clustered Psathyrella** (*Psathyrella hydrophila*) (**1**) has a moist bright brown cap drying to pale yellow, edge shaggy, unstriated. Faint ring on white stalk. Gills grayish-brown. Spores brown.

Both occur throughout North America, growing in clusters on deciduous logs, stumps and at the base of trees (*P. hydrophila*.)

Deadly Galerina and lookalikes; *M. inclinata*: reddish-brown cap and stalk, rancid smell, in clusters; numerous smaller mycenas also grow on wood.

June–Oct, Nov–Feb (Calif.); (**1**) July–Sept, Nov–March (Calif.)

DEADLY GALERINA

Galerina autumnalis   **Cap 1–2½in; stalk to 4in**

Sticky date-brown cap with striated edge is hemispherical at first, flattening out with age, and drying unevenly to a dull yellow-brown. Small ring on stalk. Spore print rust.

Cap varies from dark brown to tawny when moist. The broad adnate gills are crowded, and are at first yellowish, becoming rusty. Hollow brownish stem, blackish and with white cottony mycelium at base. **Deadly poisonous.**

Throughout North America, scattered or abundant on rotten wood of all kinds.

G. marginata: very similar, also **deadly**, cap moist not sticky; *Pholiota mutabilis*: similar, but stem sheathed in scales up to ring, in dense clusters on logs and stumps, not toxic; **Clustered Psathyrella**; **Honey Mushroom**.

October–November, May–June.

Fragile, bell-shaped, tawny brown cap is grooved from edge almost to center and the central surface is covered with minute glistening granules which soon disappear.

Gills fragile, crowded, brown to black, eventually dissolving slightly, but not so much as some other inkcaps. Edge of cap striated and often splitting as the mushroom ages. Stalk white, fragile, hollow. Spore print black.

Throughout North America, in dense clusters on stumps and logs, and on the ground in association with buried wood.

C. radians: cap covered with brown floury granules, inky gills, orange threads at base of stalk, on wet wood, often in houses; *C. disseminatus*; cap ¼–⅝in, pale gray-brown, velvety, fragile, grooved, gills not inky; **psathyrellas**.

April–October, all year in California.

Golden-yellow cap speckled with minute purplish-red scales, especially in the center. The adnexed, crowded gills are orange-yellow. Stalk yellow. Spore print white.

Although harmless, this common mushroom is not worth eating. The yellow stalk is sometimes covered with small reddish scales, and becomes hollow with age.

From Quebec to Florida in east and across USA to the West Coast, growing singly or in small groups on coniferous wood, especially pine.

Tr. decora: cap golden-yellow, only slightly speckled with black scales; *Tr. sulfureoides*: yellow-streaked cap, on coniferous logs; **tricholomas**: on ground; **Honey Mushroom**: ring on stalk, brown scales on cap.

August–November.

A bright orange fungus, becoming duller and darker with age. Cap soon flat or sunken with a central knob. Gills narrow, crowded, sharp-edged, decurrent. Pale cream spore print.

This **poisonous** fungus superficially resembles a larger version of the Chanterelle. The smooth cap eventually turns brownish. Edges of cap incurved.

Eastern North America and California, growing in clusters on deciduous trees, especially oak, and on ground in association with buried wood.

Chanterelle: fragrant, ridges not gills on underside, grows on ground; **False Chanterelle**: smaller, forked gills, grows on ground or on woody debris, associated with conifers.

July–November, November–March (Calif.)

Brownish-gray cap is streaked with darker radial fibers. Gills white, adnexed, very broad, spaced quite far apart. Stalk white, with white "roots" at base. Spores white.

The convex cap soon flattens out. Although not poisonous, it is only edible when very young. The white flesh is thin and tough with a bitter taste.

Eastern North America from Quebec to Florida, west to Iowa, growing singly on or near rotting deciduous logs and stumps, and also on ground, in association with buried wood.

Tricholomas: grow on ground; **entolomas**: pink spores; **Fawn Mushroom**: free gills, pink spores.

May–October.

HONEY MUSHROOM
Cap 1–4in; stalk to 6in   *Armillariella mellea*

1

Flattish sticky honey-colored cap has fine black hairy scales in center. Large whitish ring on stalk. Gills white, crowded, adnate or decurrent. Spore print white.

Spreads by black "bootlaces" running under bark. Edible with care. The **Big Laughing Gym** (*Gymnopilus spectabilis*) (**1**) has a velvety, rich orange-brown cap, 3¼–7in, and a thick fibrous stalk. Spores orange-brown. **Hallucinogenic**.

Throughout North America, *A. mellea* in tufts on stumps, etc., and rising from roots, a serious parasite of many trees, *G. spectabilis* in clusters at base of trees or on stumps.

A. tabescens: similar to *A. mellea*, no ring; **Scaly Pholiota; Sulfur Tuft**.

Aug–Nov, Nov–Feb (Calif.); (**1**) Aug–Oct.

SCALY PHOLIOTA

Pholiota squarrosa   **Cap 1–4in; stalk to 4in**

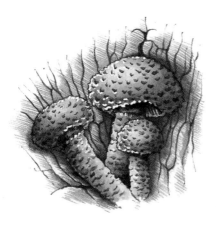

Dry yellow-brown cap and stalk are thickly covered with curled brown scales. Gills pale yellow becoming brown, adnate, crowded. Spore print brown.

The edge of the cap sometimes bears remnants of the veil which also leaves a ring or a ring-like zone on the stalk. **Poisonous**, causing gastric upsets in some people.

Widespread throughout North America, growing in clusters at the foot of deciduous trees or on stumps and logs, especially of birch or aspen.

One of several pholiotas with scaly caps and stalks growing on wood. *P. flammans*: bright yellow slimy cap; *P. aurivella*: slimy ocher cap with scales like spots; *P. squarrosoides*: sticky ocher cap, small sharp-pointed scales.

July–October.

FAWN MUSHROOM
Cap 1¼–4¾in; stalk to 4in *Pluteus cervinus*

Grayish-brown cap, sticky when wet. Gills crowded, free, white becoming pink. Stalks white, with brown fibers. Spore print salmon to brownish-pink.

Cap is bell-shaped at first, opening out flat. Flesh thick, soft, smelling faintly of radishes. Edible but only when very young, and not particularly good.

Very common and widespread throughout North America on fallen trunks, stumps, etc., especially of broadleaved trees, and on piles of sawdust.

Other *Pluteus* spp. also grow on wood, with gills white to pinkish, free, spore print pink; **entolomas**: grow on ground and have attached gills; **Platterful Mushroom**: attached white gills, white spore print.

May–October, November–May (SW.)

PEAR-SHAPED PUFFBALL

Lycoperdon pyriforme **Fruitbody to 1¾in across**

Beige or yellowish pear-shaped smoothish fruitbodies grow in clusters. Apex slightly pointed with a central pore through which the spores are released.

This is the only puffball that grows on wood. The interior spore mass is white, becoming yellowish and powdery as the spores mature. Surface covered in tiny warts. Good to eat when very young and still white throughout.

Widespread and common throughout North America on decaying stumps, fallen trunks, and buried wood.

Gem-studded Puffball; *L. echinatum*: surface covered in long spines, grows on ground in leaf litter in woods; **Pigskin Poison Puffball**: hard and leathery throughout.

July–November.

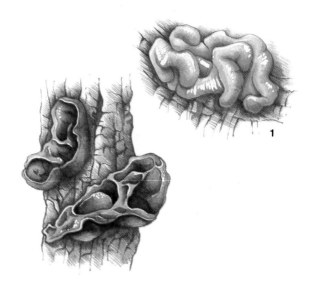

1

Ear-shaped grayish-brown to reddish-brown fruitbody has a velvety outer surface and firm rubbery flesh when young and/or moistened. The inner surface bears vein-like ridges.

The fruitbody becomes more irregularly shaped with age and is bone-hard when quite dry. Edible. **Witches Butter** (*Tremella mesenterica*) (**1**) is golden-orange, and of a softer consistency when moist, shrivelled and hard when dry.

Throughout North America, *A. auricula* mainly on coniferous wood, *T. mesenterica* on deciduous wood, especially alder, beech and oak.

T. foliacea: thin, brown, jelly-like sheets resembling a lettuce, on coniferous wood; *Dacrymyces palmatus*: bright orange lobed jelly, white attachment to wood, on conifer logs; *Exidia glandulosa*: small black contorted jellies.

May–June, September–December; (**1**) all year round.

CARBON BALLS

Daldinia concentrica   **Fruitbody ¾–1⅝in across**

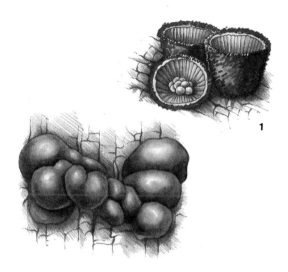

1

Hard round persistent fruitbodies, with a dull shine, at first dark brown becoming black, resembling burnt buns. When cut open they show concentric silvery rings.

This fungus often appears on dead branches after fires. **Splash Cups** (*Cyathus striatus*) (**1**) ¼–⅝in across, has a cup-shaped fruitbody (the "bird's nest") with a fluted inner surface holding 10–12 small dark "eggs" which contain spores.

D. concentrica, eastern USA west to N. Dakota, and Pacific NW, on dead wood of broadleaved trees. *C. striatus* throughout N. America, on dead and rotting wood, bark, twigs.

Exidia glandulosa: small black firm jellies. Other Bird's Nest Fungi include *Crucibulum laeve*: smooth inner wall, whitish "eggs," and *Nidularia* spp: dark eggs embedded in jelly.

June–September and over winter; (**1**) July–October.

Index and Check-list

All species in roman type are illustrated. Keep a record of your
sightings by checking the boxes

123